Basic Trut 7–

by
Bambi Betts

Illustrated by
Trevor R J Finch

GEORGE RONALD
OXFORD

George Ronald, Publisher
Oxford
www.grbooks.com

Text © Bambi Betts 1995
Illustrations © Trevor R J Finch 1995
All Rights Reserved

This edition 2015

Originally published in 1995 as three separate books:
0-85398-394-1 I Agree
0-85398-395-4 Wings of a Bird
0-85398-396-8 When I die

A catalogue record for this book is available
from the British Library

ISBN 978-0-85398-596-9

7

I Agree

Brush your teeth after you eat.

Stop on the red light,
go on the green

Don't touch the fire!

Has anyone ever said these things to you?
Do you know what they are called?

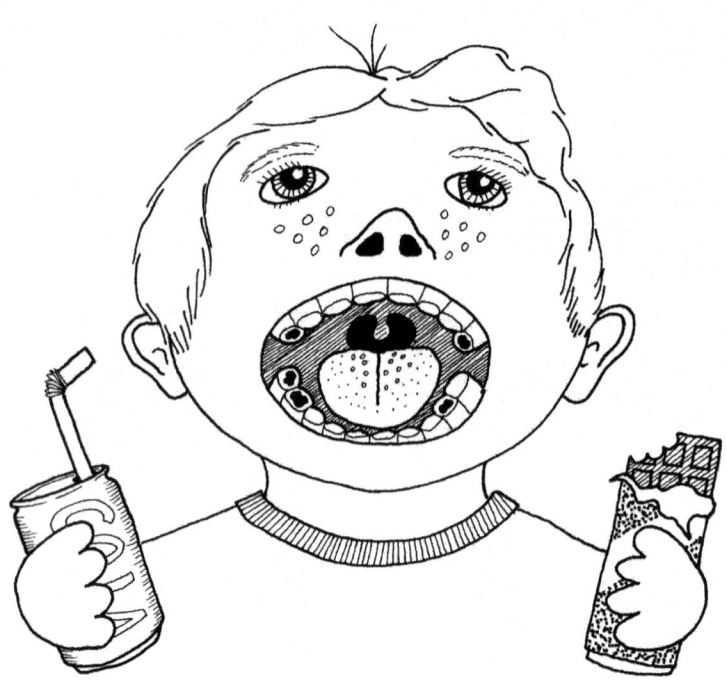

They are called rules or laws.
A rule or law is something that we must obey –
we must do what the law says.
Sometimes it is very hard to understand
why – and sometimes it is very hard to do what
the law says. But what might happen if we didn't
obey the rules?

Holes in our teeth?

A bad accident?

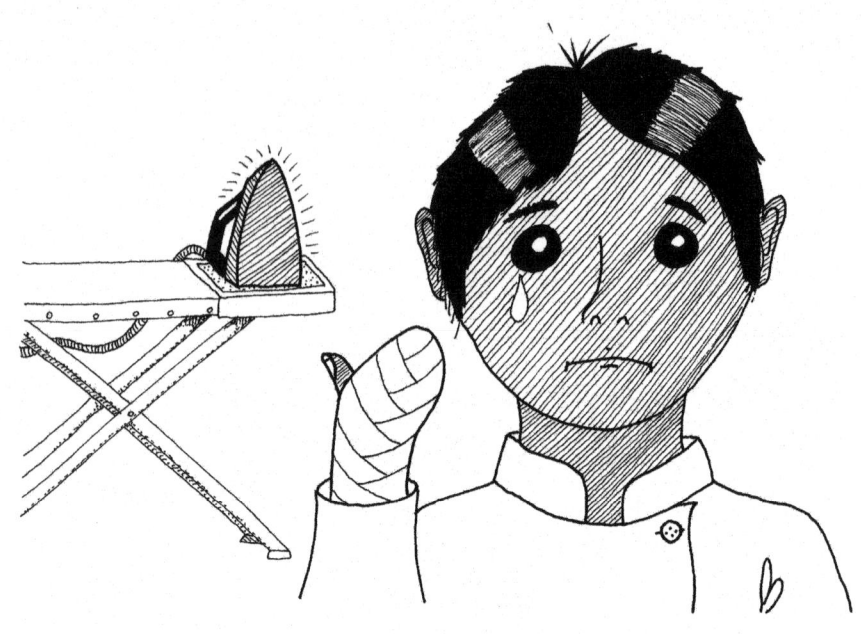

A burn?

If we don't follow the rules, there's a very good chance that we will hurt ourselves in some way.

We all agree that these rules are to protect us, to help keep us safe. Just like the rules for our homes, Bahá'u'lláh has given all people laws. Here are some of them.

Pray every day.

Learn to read and write.
Work, so that you can take care of yourself.

Go to the Bahá'í Feast every nineteen days.

Don't say bad things about others,
especially when they can't hear it.

Say no to alcohol. Say no to drugs, unless a doctor gives them to you to make you well.

Just like the rules at home, Bahá'u'lláh gave us these laws to protect us, to help keep us safe. We don't always know how these laws work. And many times it will be so hard to obey and pray every day

or get out of bed and work every day

or go to the Nineteen Day Feast each time.

But we do know that Bahá'u'lláh says that if we follow these laws we are helping our souls to grow. This means that the part that is really you – your soul – will be able to become more like God wants it to be – strong and healthy and happy.

And that is why we are here.
Do you agree?

8

Wings of a Bird

Here is a beautiful bird
flying through the sky.

It has two strong wings to help it to fly
as high and as far as it likes.

Here is another bird.
It has only one strong wing.
The other wing is not so strong.

Can this bird fly?
No. It has to stay on the ground.
A bird needs two strong wings to fly.

'Abdu'l-Bahá said that women and men, girls and boys, are like the wings of a bird.

All the women and the girls in the world
are like one wing.

All the men and the boys in the world
are like the other wing.

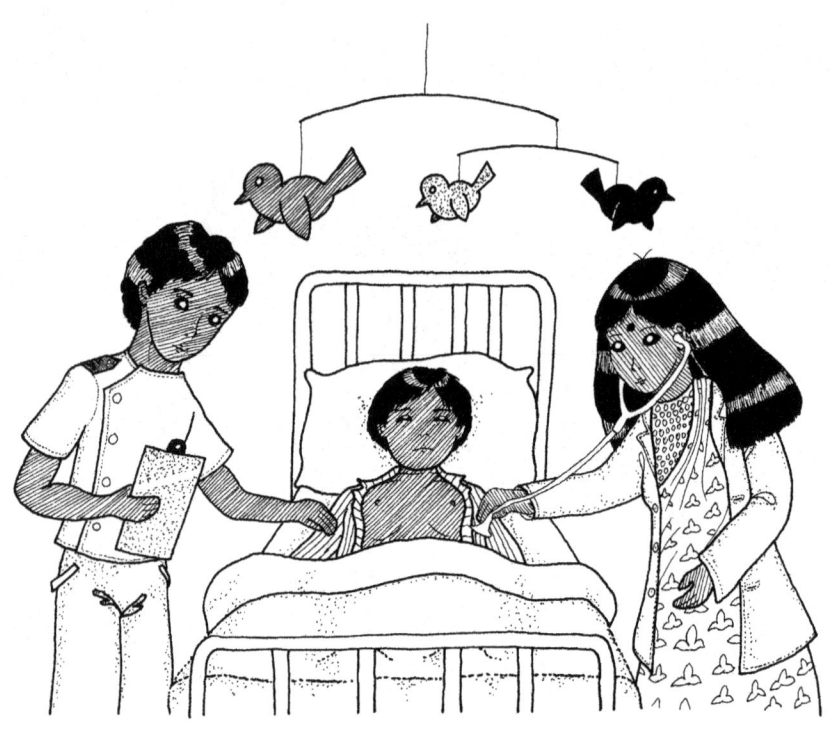

Together they are trying to make
the world a good place to live.

Sometimes women do special things
that men cannot do.

Sometimes men do things
that women find hard to do.

Usually women and men, girls and boys do the same things.

The women and girls have to be healthy
and strong in the things that they do.
The men and boys have to be healthy
and strong in the things that they do.

If the women and girls are not strong in their work, if the men and boys do not do their job

the bird cannot fly. Then no one will help the world become a better place.

Women and girls, men and boys,
all need the chance to grow and become strong
if the bird of humanity is going to fly.

9

When I Die

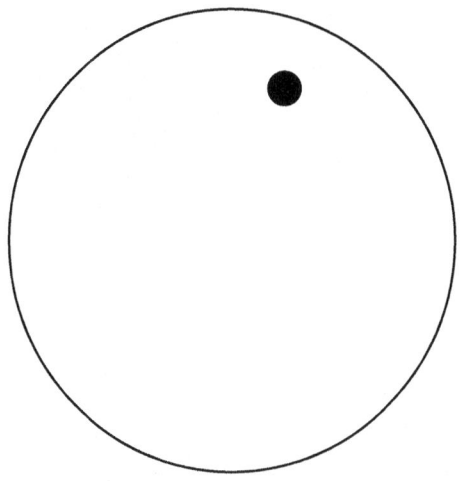

Before you were born, at the very beginning, you had no arms or legs or eyes or ears or nose or hair, or much of anything.

But as the weeks went by you grew all these things: arms and legs

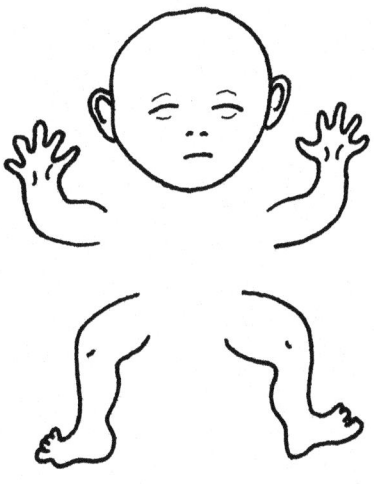

eyes and ears

until you had everything you were going to need.

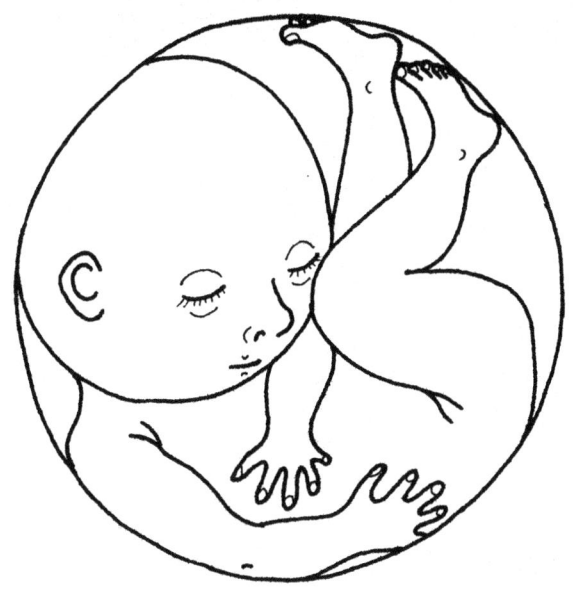

But then you grew so big inside your mother
that something had to happen.
Do you know what?

You were born!

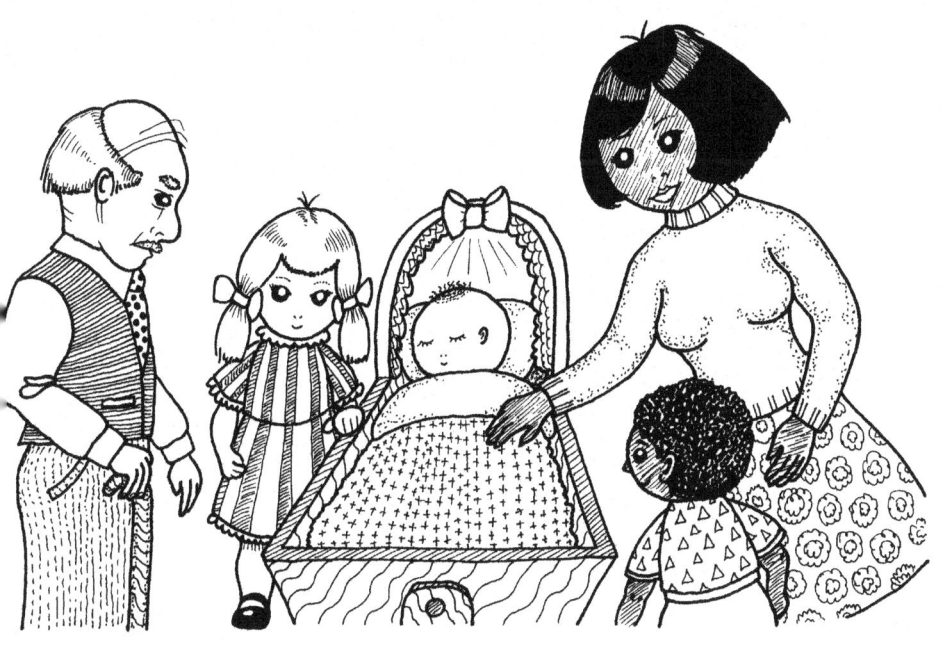

Your mother and father, family and friends were so happy to see you. They were happy because they know what an exciting place this world can be.

In this world you will grow

and grow.

One day your body will stop growing. But your soul will grow even then. Your soul is that part of you that lives on forever – the part that makes you really you. There is no picture of it because we cannot see it or touch it.

Your soul can only grow when you help it,
by praying

and thinking and planning and obeying and doing things. Your soul will learn to be patient and strong and loyal and truthful. It will know love and joy and hope.

One day your soul will no longer be able to grow within your body. Something will happen. Do you know what that is?

You will be born into another world even more wonderful than this one. There is no picture here because we cannot see that world with our eyes.

Your family and friends will miss you and feel a little sad that you have gone, but everyone will be so happy for you because you will be so much closer to God.

'From the very beginning, the children must receive divine education and must continually be reminded to remember their God.'
'Abdu'l-Bahá

Guidelines for Parents
by **Bambi Betts**

One morning, my three children and I were sitting on the bedroom floor, playing together. We had just returned home the night before from a Bahá'í conference. Quite suddenly, the four-year-old said, 'At the conference they told us that mankind is one.'

'That's true,' she continued, 'if mankind is one, then when will it be two?' Many parents have experienced the sweetness and humour of such misperceptions in their young children. They enrich the family culture and become endearing tales for the grandchildren. However, as parents we have the awesome responsibility to transmit to our children the basic truths concerning existence. It is all too easy to read a story or give a short lesson to a child and assume that because we understand the message (i.e. mankind is one), that the child does as well. If mankind is to progress toward the creation of a better civilization, and individuals toward the refinement of spiritual qualities, this responsibility cannot be left to chance. Like all other aspects of development, it requires care and attention consistent with the needs, capacities and perceptions of each particular phase of development.

The Báb assures us that even the youngest of children today will be wiser than the wisest man of past generations. Again, this will not happen by chance. The Basic Truths Series is designed to assist you in providing the basic vocabulary and concepts needed to begin the process of ensuring that the words become firm concepts, consistent with reality as well as relevant to your child's current perception of life. Obviously, none of the books is intended to be a thorough discussion of the topic, rather a gentle introduction to the world of concepts from the viewpoint of a young child.

Most parents will know their own child well enough to make the best use of these books. However, so that each of you does not feel he must re-invent the wheel, a few ideas from other parents might prove useful.

1. Follow the child's lead. Let him stop you and ask questions or make comments. Simply by listening you will pick up valuable clues about his level of understanding.
2. The illustrations are an integral part of learning for young children. Use them to bring the concept closer to the child's own experience.
3. Whenever possible, use examples from the child's daily life to make a point come alive.
4. Remind the child often that these ideas came from Bahá'u'lláh.
5. Ask the child to tell you about the book after you've read it. A young child will typically focus on one illustration or one part which is close to his own experience. This is another useful tool for determining the level of his comprehension.